Wisdom Rising

Poems and Writings for Heart Directed Living

JIM PETERSON

I

To Caroline, Sonia, and Michelle
for guiding me to
the Path of The Heart.

Cover Photo by
J Dickerson

ISBN-13: 978-1499630367
ISBN-10: 1499630360

TABLE OF CONTENTS

a

Acknowledgements

I extend considerable gratitude to my wife Glenda and the many dear friends who have encouraged me and supported the creation of this book.

Introduction

I remember with absolute clarity the moment a poem first came to me early in 2005. I was vacuuming our living room rug when the opening lines to a poem came into my awareness and I knew who the poem was for. I turned off the vacuum, went to my computer to write the first line of the poem, and the rest came forward.

Strangely none of this seemed out of the ordinary at the time. It just felt so natural and I knew with absolute clarity that the poem did not spring from my intellect. Its origin was from wisdom deep within me, a spiritual source I was just beginning to accept, and what I now call my Inner Wisdom or simply Spirit. But there are other names for this source of wisdom: The Ascended Masters, Christ, The Holy Spirit, The angels and archangels, Creator, or simply our spirit guides. What I have come to realize is that they are all reflections of the Divine Voice that resides in each of us. It is the aspect of our self that remembers God and calls us back to the awareness that we are not only worthy of God's Love but that we are one with the Creator. There are no exceptions.

I discovered early on, as more poems started coming forward, the over arching experience of each was peace and clarity. The teachings that spring from the poems are always affirming, gentle, and heart centered. By this I mean that the teachings do not lead to the thinking mind (intellect) but rather inward where truth is simply known upon its hearing.

The first poems to come through me were guidance for others. Some poems were for friends and some for people I hardly knew. However, they also contained teachings that were meaningful for me. In all cases I sent the poem on to the person for which it was meant. As I became practiced in receiving and writing out these wisdom writings, I started to feel a desire to more fully express what was in my Heart. We are constantly surrounded by the expressions of Love but often we are attuned to the discontent that seems to fill our lives. The poems opened me up to a greater awareness of the love that is in my heart and to the expressions of love that are literally everywhere. They came through interactions with not only the people in my life but with all living things.

Next I found that I could receive answers to questions and problems. As I moved along my spiritual path I came to many points where I had to leave behind old ways of thinking, believing, and acting. I found these could be difficult times, for while the old ways no longer serve, the new ways were not yet fully formed. This form of Wisdom writing quickly became a way for me to get answers, guidance and clarity during these confusing times. There were other times where I simply wanted to know things on a deeper level. I would go to my Heart Center and ask for clarity and allow the wisdom to come forward through my writing. Some of these writings came as poems and others came as a dialogue between me and Spirit. Chapter V contains many of these writings.

As my Heart opened to the expressions of Love that seemed increasingly pervasive, I began to experience others in different, more meaningful ways. As another would be telling me of the discontent in their lives, I began to experience a deeper sense of their true selves. It might come as energy emanating from their physical body that I could only describe as healing and loving. Sometimes it was a knowing that the discontent they were projecting was nothing more than a veil which blocked them from the awareness of their innocent and loving nature. Sometimes what I sensed was in conflict with my own judgments about the person. In such cases I asked for clarity and a poem would come forward that would allow me to see them more truly. Some of the poems that came to me I shared, as I was gently compelled to do so by Spirit, and others were meant as teachings for me. They showed how my judgments of others could be based on old biases and superficial observations that cloud my ability to see truly and that when I set these aside, truth and clarity can shine through.

Finally, this Heart opening has also allowed me to experience messages from those who have died and on occasion children yet to be born who wish to communicate to loved ones who reside within this physical world. These messages come to me as poems and collectively they have given me a glimpse of what it is like for them on "the other side". These poems are contained in Chapter IV.

You will find that throughout this work I use the word Heart and occasionally Heart Center. I have been asked if I am referring to the body's heart or the spiritual heart. I am actually referring to an experience and a state of being. We are in physical form thus our experiences tend to be felt within our body. We are all familiar with the experiences of Peace, Joy, Love, Affirmation, and Gratitude. When I ask my students where they experience these states most often they say in the chest or heart area. I have come to recognize that what we are actually experiencing is a state of being that is beyond our analytical mind and physical body. It is a sense of joining. The joining can be with another or any or all aspects of that which surrounds us.

I have found that when we consciously open ourselves to this state of being we connect to a wisdom that is not of our intellect. What we are experiencing in these moments is the movement to our true state of being, the experience of our divine self and our unfettered connection to Source – The Divine.

I am not a perfect channel to Spirit's voice. I still have an intact and quite vocal ego, thus distortion to some extent is inevitable. Given this, I ask that as you read the writings that follow, listen with your Heart. Those things which are heart opening take in and allow the resonance of the words to speak to you. Simply rest with the experience of these words without thought or judgment and let Spirit speak directly to you.

Conversely, you may come to words or phrasings that are confusing, or trigger feelings of discontent. I refer to these experiences as heart closing. These words are not worthy of your attention. Let them go and move on to that which inspires and moves you. That part of us that believes we are not worthy of God's love will try to divert our attention to that which closes our heart in order to distract us from truth. Be vigilant for peace rather than discontent. Do not buy into the inner struggle. Rather see the struggle as merely a choice to attend to that which moves you rather than that which distracts you.

Even though the poems and wisdom writings that follow chronicle my spiritual path and that of others in my life, know that in truth they were also written for you. We are all joined and there is no such thing as individual inspiration. All share in the inner work. Some of the writings may not resonate for you but many will. Experience the words and let them take you to your Inner Wisdom.

Chapter I
The Two Voices

We are each on a path to spiritual enlightenment and within each of us is the wisdom that will guide us along our unique path. This wisdom lies within our Intuitive or Heart Center, the gateway to our spiritual essence. Our intuition is the voice of our true spiritual selves – our Higher Self.

For much of our lives we believe we are using our free will in the choices we make but many of us are locked into a life where we have given up our free will. We are slaves to the voice of our fears, our anger, and our discontent. We are robots that merely react as life seemingly throws us one random challenge after another. Oh, there are times of happiness but this happiness is short-lived because it is built on a foundation of fear and anger. These emotions left unresolved are corrosive to our quality of life, to our ability to manifest a lasting joy, the core of our true nature.

We have two sources of inner guidance. The first is that part of us that I call the fearful mind or the fearful ego. We all know it. It is that part of us that tends to perceive only the threat in things. It also works to set ourselves apart as better than or worse than others. This part seeks allies to improve or uphold a position, but does not seek brothers or sisters who will see us through loving eyes. This is because deep down the fearful ego believes we are not worthy of happiness. Thus the message of our fearful mind is critical, demanding, and fills us with anxiety. This anxiety is often projected outward as anger and inward as depression. It keeps us off-balance, defensive, and often confused. The fearful mind does not bring answers but only questions, doubts, and conflicting judgments (good vs. evil) that lock us into a never ending inner debate of what is truth and the right course of action.

The other source of inner guidance is our intuition, our conduit to what I call our Inner Wisdom. As I mentioned in the introduction, there are many terms for this source of guidance: the Higher Self, Spirit, God/Goddess, spirit guides, angels, Ascended Masters, etc. I often use the term "true intuition" or "Heart Centered intuition"

1

because our fearful mind likes to masquerade as intuition. It is amazingly simple to differentiate true intuition from the false intuition of the fearful ego. True intuition is affirming, loving, clarifying, and centering. This source of guidance answers questions asked of it. This is unlike the fearful ego that raises questions and keep us locked in an internal debate.

The following pages contain poems that came to me as teachings and affirmations as I consciously explored the nature of these two voices.

For This I am Grateful

You have taught me to follow my Heart.
To trust the Voice Within.

At times this is hard, for Your voice is new
and I do not always understand.
While the voice of my fears
is familiar and all too clear.

As I have asked, so too have you provided
the experiences and beloved teachers
that have helped attune me to Your message.
For This I am Grateful.

Your Teachers have shown me
through example and experience
how to more fully trust and love myself;
How to know Your guidance in its many forms,
by attuning myself to Your calm and loving vibration.
For This I am Grateful.

Your Teachers have deepened my awareness
of the intuitive gifts which connect me
to my brothers and sisters and to You.
When I touch the Soul of my brother and sister
My heart sings with joy for I know them
and in that moment I know You.

We are all One.
I am at peace.

For this I am grateful

February 2006

The Two Voices

Follow your Heart.
You are a Child of God.
You know what to do.

The arguing voice is that of fear.
It leads only to unhappiness.
This is the path of pain.

Quiet your mind and go to
your place of calmness.
your Heart.

The voice of your Heart does not argue.
The voice of your Heart guides and
will answer your questions.

Learn to go inward
and formulate questions
not problems.

I Am with you – always.

Truth is within you.
Seek your Truth.
You will know truth
by the joy it brings you in the
moment it is remembered.

This is the Path of The Heart.
The Path of Joy.
You are ready.
Seek the Path of Joy.

May 12, 2006

The Heart of Now

The Heart of Now is my path.
I shall not wander.

As the hummingbird is drawn to
the morning blossom,
I follow the soothing rhythm
of the Voice Within.

There are many distractions,
which only lead me
to discontent.

But I know their vibration
and I have chosen
for the Voice of My Heart.
For the Voice of God.

I shall not wander.

January 19, 2008

Peace Expands

Ah! My Singing Heart,
it is always there in the background.

I can feel it.
But often it goes unnoticed.

It is a sweet melody
of peace,
of Being.

It is a filling.
A sensation of completeness.

It is obscured by the thinking mind.
For it searches for more within the physical,
in vain.

I am old in years and fortunately wiser.
I have obtained that which I sought
within the world.
It brought me many things,
but not peace.

Even through all the searching and achieving
I knew not what I sought.
Except perhaps
the false dreams of others.

But Wisdom brought me teachers
who lead me to my Heart.

Now desire springs from this place of creation.
It is The Heart's Desire I seek now.

I know where it lies.

I remove distractions. There are many.
But with each one gone
Peace expands.

January 19, 2008

Awakening

I know the many doubts
that spring from unknown places.

They are thoughts without meaning.
Except that which I offer.

I have come to recognize
this inner voice.
It is not my voice.
It is part of me
but only as a dream
is of the dreamer.

It is a voice that tells me of
past hurts and future fears.

It is a voice that only lives
in the dream.

It fears awakening and its destruction.
So it masquerades as me.

I am fooled no longer.

I choose awakening.

March 14, 2008

Peace

Peace.
I know You.

There is a place
within me
where your presence
dwells.

Thoughts and emotions
rage above it.

But Peace
is undisturbed.

Joy spreads
across my awareness.

For an instant
I am free.
From this body.
This thinking mind
I call me.

August 25, 2008

Wisdom Rising

Wisdom awaits our choice.
There seem to be many choices
and they appear to come from all directions.

In our waking life and in our dreams.

But in reality there is one choice
masquerading as many.

In every moment of every day
we merely choose between truth and falsehood.

Between what our thinking mind tells us
and what we know in our Heart as Truth.

It is personified in the struggle
between past perceptions
and current experience.

Within the past is deception and discontent.
The present moment is the domain of Wisdom.

Truth or the right course of action
is known in the moment.
It is beyond the workings of the intellect.
It is simply experienced and known as Truth.

We can resist Truth and choose falsehood.
But only for a while.

Falsehood always brings pain
and eventually you will seek another way.
Another voice to guide you.

You will know the voice of Truth
in the moment it arises
into your awareness.

It is Wisdom calling
It is a call you know well
but have left unattended.
But no longer.

December 12, 2013

Chapter II
Building a Foundation
for True Self-Awareness

The foundation upon which our spiritual awakening rests is Love. It is both the path and the State of Being which awaits us at the end of our journey. I have found that the awareness of Love cannot expand without first nurturing love of self. As I look back on my own path I find three practices: Gratitude, Affirmation, and Intention, which more than anything else helped me connect to the love that is within me. These practices and writings which guided me came in a particular order and I am presenting them in this way. However, they are different forms of the expression of love and in particular love of self. Thus one is not more important than the other.

Gratitude as a Foundation for True Self-Awareness

While gratitude is often thought of as thankfulness directed at something or someone outside of our self, it is actually an expression of self-love, for what we give to others we also receive. It has long been known that little self-growth can occur without self-love. But for someone trapped in their painful emotions, self-love can be a hard reach while gratitude can be an easier step. For me I have found that even in the most difficult of times there are experiences and things in my life for which I am grateful. By keeping these experiences alive within us we are actually directing love back to our self.

The Artist's Prayer

As our Hearts open
We sense Your presence.

We know You.

You are the deep Knowing that is of the Heart.

Thoughts and experiences that we put into words are
not adequate to describe the peace of Your Knowing.

Our art knows You
for it comes from our remembrance of who You are
and that we are all one with You.

We are Your sons and daughters.
Our art is the expression
of a child's love for their Father.

Art is our gift to our brothers and sisters
to remind them from where they came
and to guide them
and us back to the beginning.

We are at peace.
We know You.

2005

Grandfather

Grandfather,
I have come such a long way.
Yet I feel lost.

I search for you - for who I am in the past.
I find meaning there but it is old and does not serve me now.

I search the future but I cannot see.

I search the now and there you are.
You are in my Heart.

I walk a new path with new lessons.
It is the path of the Heart.

Your teachings have brought me to this new place.
It is a place of creation
and my Heart is the instrument of creation.
You are wise – guide me in this new power
that I may use it as a means to light my path of return and that of
my brothers and sisters.

Grandfather,
I have come a long way.
I can see my path.

I am Grateful.

February 6, 2006

Jeff's Song

Brother where are you?
Oh, there you are.
You are in my heart.
I loved you before the first day.

Joy is our birthright and this is
our gift to each other.
Our joy is love turned to play.
We know the joy of being,
the joy of sharing,
the joy of helping,
and the joy when we touch
each other's Soul.

You are my brother
and I have had the joy
of being your guide.

But you have also been my guide.
You lead me to the awareness
of God in my life.
You awaken my inner child who is
the gate keeper of my magical self.

Yes, you are in my heart.
You bring joy to my life.
I am grateful.

February 23, 2006

Our Hearts Are One

My Heart sings.
I have touched the Spirit of
My brothers and sisters.

I sense the song in their Hearts.
I know they are guided.
I know the peace of the Heart.
Touching their Hearts
is my reminder.

This is my gift.
This is my path of return.
What I give is
what I receive.

My tears are that of Joy.
The Joy of touching their Truth.
For it is also my Truth.
They are tears of affirmation;
There is only one Heart
splintered by illusion;
There is only one Truth
hidden by our fears.

When I touch another's Heart
I see the illusion.
I know the fears as false idols.
I see their joyful Hearts
and in this I know my Heart
for it is our Heart.

Our Hearts are One.

May 12, 2006

Father

As I quiet my mind
I go to You.
I go in peace and love;
With the certainty
of your Love.

I go quietly.
I have no worldly demands
or needs.
Only the desire to be with You.
To feel You surround me.

I speak the word,
"Father"
and my awareness returns
to my true place.
A place I have never left.
The joy brings soft tears
of remembrance
and affirmation.

I am Your son.
I have lived in the illusion
of our separation.

The illusion is still strong,
but it is weakening.
I know Truth
and it guides me.

I follow joy.
It is Your call to me.
It illuminates my path.

Thank You Father.

August 5, 2006

17

The Light Within

I lived in the darkness.
But I always felt
the Light within me.

It revealed itself
in the wonder and innocence
that has always been
part of my being.

But I saw these as weaknesses:
The wonder within was mistaken for
dreams of fantasy and magic
that seemed to distract me from worldly goals.

Innocence was construed as gullibility
for it seemed to make me an easy target
for the discontent of others.

I sought freedom from inner doubts
by seeking outward
for my salvation - my identity.

I sought approval and recognition
through superficial relationships,
thrills, and drinking buddies.

But others saw the light within me;
the innocence rooted in an infectious optimism
that sought solutions not blame
and the wonder that could turn drudgery
into play.

These believing eyes helped me
see myself more truly
and nurtured the gifts that would guide me
though a life of service and ultimately
to inner peace.

Even when I could not see myself truly
others did and through their eyes
the path to my true self
was illuminated.

September 7, 2009

Companions

I go within.
I find each of you there.
You are companions
on a great journey.

It is a journey to
clarity,
purpose,
oneness.

I feel the Love
that dwells
in each of you.

It is Love
calling to Love.

It illuminates
my path.

When Hearts connect
there can only be peace.

You are my blessing.
I am at peace.

September 13, 2009

Christ

Christ stands beside me
for I have yet to fully accept
that he is my True Self.

I feel his presence
like the warmth of the sun
on a summer morning.

His gentle hands
reach out to guide me.
To assure me.
I am not on a solitary path.

His image is obscured
by the Light that envelops him.
His gift is Peace.
His presence Wonder.
His essence Love.

He has shown me
the truth
of who and what I am.

He has led me
to the experience
of our Father.

He is
My Brother,
My Guide,
My Heart,
My Self.

December 23, 2009

Divine Mother

I feel Your presence.
I know it is but an echo
of my remembrance.

But it fills me
with Wonder,
but above all
Peace.

I am but a small child
cradled in Your arms
and nurtured by
Your Love.

Contentment
permeates my consciousness.

Innocence
is my State of Being.

I am filled
beyond wanting.

Discontent is a word
without meaning.

Your Love
is the beacon
to which I have
long journeyed.

I know You
for all the things
I have made
and experienced
reflect some aspect
of your Grace

I am Your Son.
Gratitude and Love
are my gifts to You.

December 24, 2009

The River

The river flows gently onward.
Along grassy meadows and
gently rolling hills.

It is the river of our journey.
It has passed through its turbulent birth
in the high and majestic mountains.

It has carved stone to make its path.
It has found its way to calm waters
which celebrate its long journey to peace.

We journey to the sea of our awakening.
I feel the growing calmness and peace
that flows from our relationship.

We are the river.
I celebrate our journey.
A journey to peace and joy.

May 8, 2011

Ask and It is Given

My Heart overflows with Joy.

I do not know whether to laugh or cry.
I realize both are expressions of the same experience.
Connection to Source – The Spirit Within.

Confusion is gently melting away.
I asked and it was given.

In many forms it came;
Inspirational writing,
reaching out to loved ones,
innocent conversations with neighbors
and even strangers.

A phone call from my son.
Our roles reversed.
He was the believing eyes
and I was the one in doubt.

The Holy Spirit was present in all these experiences.
I felt it in my heart and in every fiber of my being.

Peace and joy are with me.
There is still more to learn and
beliefs of unworthiness to clear.

I thought I had lost my path but
Spirit showed me the folly of such thoughts.

Ask and it is given is not a notion but a promise.
I am learning this on a deeper and deeper level.
Spirit Guides me.

I am grateful.

October 9, 2012

Self-Affirmation as a Foundation for True Self-Awareness

In its pure form, self-affirmation is an expression of the Heart and as such it is an expression of self-love that connects us to others (people, animals, plants, nature, and our spiritual guides). The affirmation I speak of is not related to "pride" or "self esteem" which too often reflects the attempts to build our self-image by setting our self apart from others. We are conditioned in so many ways to keep our attention on the problems and negative things in our lives. We do not see the ways that we are dynamically connected to our surroundings (both physical and nonphysical). We are not passive recipients of our experience – but rather co-creators. I have come to learn that what we experience is influenced by how we think and thus feel about our self and the world around us. When we think negatively, what we experience is negative. In this way we attune our self to the pain in our lives and thus what we see in the world reflects this back and obscures our true nature.

The alternative lies in seeing and honoring the multitude of experiences which tell us of our true nature. These affirming experiences lie in the heart to heart connections we make with others in large and small ways. They lie in the synchronicities that tell us we are guided. The intuitive hits that come true which remind us that we have relational powers that are still untapped. These are the experiences that expand the awareness of our Heart; they are windows into our true self and as such need to be celebrated. For in celebrating them we acknowledge and honor our selves. Eventually we come to realize that we are worthy of happiness, that we are never alone, and that we are guided.

My Higher Self Calls

You honor Me
when you create from your
Heart.

Do not be afraid.
I am with you.
You know this for
you have felt My presence.

I am the Joy.
I am the pure pleasure in
Being.
I am the Melody.
I am your Singing Heart.
I am Truth.
I am the Voice of God.
I am your
True Spiritual Self.

I connect you to
All That Is.

You are a Child of the Light.
Joy is your birthright.
Do not be afraid.
I am with you.
I am the joy in
your heart.
Follow your joy
for it alone illuminates
your spiritual path.

March 25, 2006

The Guardian's Song

The time is at hand.
Your voice sings of Truth
but has been silent.
It is a song of
the Heart.

Claim your joy
not your pain.
I am with you
and will be
your guide.

I am the joy in
your Heart.
The pain is a mask
which hides Me
and your
True Self.

It is time to move with
the melody of your Heart.
The time is at hand.

March 27, 2006

Conversation with Christ

It is time
for your awakening.

I know Your voice.
It is the voice of my first awakening.
I know Your voice
by the joy
it brings me.

Follow my teachings.
They are the teachings of the Heart.
Your physical mind leads you only to uncertainty.
Your Heart leads you to Truth.
Follow the joy of your Heart.
Your Heart will lead you to Me.

As I silence my mind I turn to my Heart
and find you there.
The joy is almost overwhelming.

That is because it is new.
Do not be afraid because once found
you can never lose the connection to me.
True Joy is your birthright.
You are the son of God
and I am your brother.
I have come to lead you back
to our Father.

Yes, it is time for my awakening.
I am ready.
You are in my Heart
and my Heart sings with Joy.
I am Grateful.
It is time.

March 2006

The Light Within

The Light is within.
Your path is unfolding.
You are guided.
You are loved.
You shine.

Owl guides you
and illuminates your path.

You are not the field mouse
that must hide in the shadow.

You are the owl.
You know the shadow.
But it is not a place you need to fear.
You have the gift of clear vision.
Look through the fear,
Look through the shadow,
and there you will find
your joy.

You are guided.
You shine.
Trust in this.

October 9, 2006

The Keeper

You seek the grassy plains
of peace and harmony.
Not as the predator
but as the Keeper.

This is your domain.
You are The Keeper.
Clarity of sight is your gift.
Claim your power.

The belief in weakness is the illusion.
Use your sense – Your sixth sense.
Like gazelle your senses
are attuned to
differentiating that which brings life
and that which takes life.

You have learned the wisdom of
pursuing that which is life-giving
and moving swiftly beyond
that which is life-taking.

Do not let fear
cloud your vision.
Like Gazelle
know fear as your friend.
Move into it and past it
and clarity will be yours.

Seek your domain.
You are The Keeper.

October 22, 2006

31

The Peace of God

We are whole and complete.

When I quiet my mind
I know the truth of this.

I feel Your presence in every
breath I take.
In every beat of my heart.

I feel my brothers and sisters.
I sense their agony and struggle.
But I also know this is not
who they are.

I feel the peace of God
and it is here where my Spirit
and that of my brothers and sisters
are joined as One.

We live in a world
we have made to hide our shame.
We believe we have offended
our Father.
That we have sought Peace
outside His presence.

But we are with Him
but lost in an illusion.

Quiet your mind.
Go to your Heart.
You will find God there.
You will knowTruth
by the Peace
that fills you.

January 8, 2007

The Gardener

Your beauty is captured
in the flowers you nurture.
They are a reflection of your Spirit.

They are the symbol
of your radiance.
They are a sign of your purpose.

You manifest beauty
in all that you touch.
It surrounds you.
It is time to accept the
beauty that is within you.

Release the time of doubting.
You are the gardener.
Your touch
brings life.
Your care
brings beauty.
Your love
brings Light.

May 13, 2007

The Storm Rages

The storm rages.
It is the seat of our discontent.

The storm is of our making.
It is our fear and belief
that we are not worthy.

But there are always signs of peace:
There is the light of the sun that shines
even after the darkest of nights;
The wildflowers that blossom
even after the coldest of winters.

There is even love
in the harshest of rains,
the tears of our discontent
which nourish and cleanse
the beauty that surrounds us.

These too are of our making.
It is the part of us that remembers
who we are:

That we are Children of the Light;
That we are One with God;
That we are worthy;
That the storm is a dream
from which we have already awoken.

This awareness lies in our Hearts,
the seat of our spiritual self.
It is from here that the beauty of
the world we have made springs forth.

It is our reminder that
the essential nature of God is Love,
That true creation springs from Love,
That we were made in God's image.
That Joy is our birthright.

All else is illusion.

August 23, 2008

Owl Speaks

I speak to you through the mist
of your dream.

My message is one of clarity.
You have a gift.
It is an aspect of your True Self.

Wisdom flows from you like the waters
of a crystal clear spring
emerging into the light of day.

You have attuned yourself
to this wisdom.
But you fear it is of your making.

Be at peace.
The Memory of God,
Your True Self guides you.

You are awakening.
You have sensed the Light
which is the canvas upon which
the physical world subsists.

Your presence guides others.
You teach because this is your nature.
It connects you to others.
It removes the barriers
that have been erected
which seem to separate yourself
from your brothers and sisters.

Your ego takes part in your teaching.
But your Heart is strong.
You take the lessons of the ego
and use them to remove the barriers
to Truth.

Teach,
Love,
be The Light
that you are.

June 27, 2009

Lead Into Gold

Your journey
is one of peace.

You seek
the calm waters
that flow from
your Heart.

There are
many distractions:
Career,
Security,
Relationship.

They draw on you
like the desert draws
heat from the sun.

But you are an alchemist.
You are learning to turn
opposition into opportunity,
confusion into intention,
conflict into harmony.

Take the lead of discontent
and shape it into the gold
of your Heart's desires.

January 9, 2010

The Path of the Heart

The great mysteries
of the forest and the mountains
are unlocked before you.

You walk a path
filled with life and wonder.

You are guide and follower.
What you give you receive.

Your journey is one of joining and being.

The mist has surrounded you
but it is thinning.

The mist is the mystery
only because it dims your sight.

But the great beauty
that surrounds and fills you
is no longer hidden.

True sight is yours.
You know the way.

You guide others.
In this way you find
truth and oneness.

Be at peace.
You walk the path
of the Heart.

2011

Love Expands

Love expands.
In this physical world
its signs are everywhere.
But it is in the relationship with your self
that Love's presence is truly experienced.

You have walked through your fears
into wisdom.
You are a teacher of God.
You know this.

You are reaching for
the Mind of God.
It is within you.
You know this.

Seek the Love that fills you
and teach from this place.
It is your passion
that will guide you
to the Mind of God.

On this physical plane
Heartfelt love from others
surrounds you.
Use this love to reflect back
the Love that fills them.

Use the love extended to you
to heal their fears.
To guide them to Love's Presence
within themselves.

You are a Teacher of God
and He is well-pleased.

January 23, 2012

Time Collapses

The dream is ending.
Time is collapsing.

You have all done your service.
More is to come and
Love guides you.

Like water flowing to the ocean
I am the channel that guides your flow.
Like drops of rain
other brothers and sisters will join you.

You are a force that will forge
through stone and muck.

Your path can no longer be blocked.
An infinite ocean of love awaits
you, your brothers and sisters.

It is a place you flow to
but have never left.

Time is collapsing
your joy can no longer be contained
by the dream.

October 8, 2012

The Dance

We dance as One.

The Light swirls
enveloping our every movement,
each dip into joy and wonder.

Our Hearts soar as we move with the rhythm
of our journey to Knowledge.

We are brothers and sisters together
in a reunion of intention.

We seek the calm waters of Your Being.
We know where It lies;
In our joining.

Our Hearts expand with each sharing,
With each laugh and tear of remembrance.

Fear is ending.
Its holy purpose fulfilled.

The Dance only knows joy and peace.
All else is illusion.

June 21, 2013

Love's Path

I am learning to move
to the rhythm of Your Love.

I can feel Its flow
between all things
even in this illusory world
we seem to occupy.

It draws me like
A hummingbird to nectar.

It does not rise and fall
as so many things do
in this physical world.

It is always there.
Only my awareness wanes.

I know now that It is eternal.
It extends beyond death.
It is not a force but a
State of Being.

When I attune myself to
This ever-present flow of Love
I find wisdom and clarity.

I see beneath
the veil we project to hide our fears
and the stories we weave
to mask our sadness.

The joy in my heart
is almost overwhelming
for It can no longer be contained
by this physical body.

Joy extends into infinity
along with my awareness.
I glimpse a mere fragment of
our True Self.

It is enough for now
but I have touched the truth
of who we are
and I can no longer hide
in the illusion.

I have chosen awakening
My path is irrevocable.

June 22, 2013

Love Flows

I see the movement of Love.
It surrounds us.
There is no place it is not.

Even in the harshest of arguments.
It is our desire to be worthy of love
that misguides us.

Our movement to Love's awareness
is the only driving force we ever face.
Fear is not a force it is merely the lack of faith.
A belief in something that is not real.

But the flow of Love is ever-present.
Awareness of it is rekindled by
the most innocent of events;

an infant's smile,

a sweet melody,

the kind gesture
of a stranger,

the gentle caress of
a loved one,

the sound of
water flowing over rocks.

Love is not a choice
for it is at the heart of our nature.

What we choose is
to attune our self (or not)
to its presence.

September 7, 2013

Intention as a Foundation for True Self-Awareness

Much is known and has been written about intention. It is a powerful and essential tool for manifesting. Bringing into our life the things we desire. Although we are spiritual beings much of our awareness is tied to our physical world. Thus, we most often focus our intention on physical things such as a better car, a better job, better health. While these things can contribute to a more comfortable life, I have found that it is the quality of my internal experience that most impacts the quality of my life. All things in the physical world change; they evolve and eventually they decay. Thus it is a shaky foundation upon which to set our happiness.

We can also form our intentions from a place of fear and scarcity. From this place, our wanting arises from a belief that others have what we lack: the perfect home, the ideal mate, or a higher paying job. When we attempt to manifest from a place of scarcity we draw to our self scarcity. When we tie our happiness to external factors discontent will eventually prevail. Even if we should gain what we seek, the foundation of our seeking is based in fear and scarcity and these states will inevitably prevail.

The form of intention contained in the following poems springs from the heart. While the heart is an instrument of joining our fears are the instrument of separation. It is in the pursuit of a quality of life that connects us to our true nature and the world around us that will lead to true joy. We are powerful manifestors who can bring into our lives whatever it is we focus adequate attention on. Thus it is important that we continually challenge our self to reach into our hearts and ask for what will bring true peace and joy.

All Else Is Illusion

It is time for my rebirth.
I seek the calm waters of my Spirit.
The purity of the Heart.
The Knowing that is not of the physical mind.
These I find in the experience of the Heart:

Truth and joy are inseparable.
They are my birthright
All else is illusion.

As I search my Heart.
I find my brothers and sisters.
The love that is of the Heart
knows not exclusion.
We are One.
All else is illusion.

I search my Heart
and I find God.
Our time is at hand.
It is time for our return to his side.
A place we never left.
All else is illusion

I search my heart
And I feel God's Love.
We are his beloved children
In whom he is well pleased.
All else is illusion.

2006

48

Journey of Surrender

We all flow in a single direction.
It is back to the full awareness
of who we are.

As surely as we perceive the rising sun,
we are guided on this journey of return.

It is a journey of surrender.

We are trapped in our fears,
which are illusion.
But even in the darkness of our fears
our Heart still illuminates the way.

We are the Sons and Daughters
of God.

Our true nature is Love
and it is Love that guides us.

We have come to believe
we are separated from God.

But this is illusion.
We are still at his side.
Our awareness is drawn to this Truth
and it is Love that illuminates
our path.

On this path of enlightenment – The Path of Joy,
you need not surrender anything
but your fears.

August 31, 2006

The Search

I feel Your presence.

I have been lost in my own mind.
I searched for You there
but only found confusion.

Now I search for Peace
and there is where
I find You.

It is a lesson
many times learned.
But each time
on a deeper level.

Guide me
until finally
there are
no more levels.

Only Oneness.

May 21, 2007

Guide Me

The Way is before me.
It is not hidden
except by my fears and doubts.

Guide me in seeing through
and beyond the illusions
I have made.

Guide me in facing and releasing
the demons of my mind
which bind me
to judgment and discontent.

Remind me of the Love
that is your presence within me always.

I know where you dwell.
I can reach it at will.
But my awareness
does not linger there.
I am easily distracted.
Guide me in removing
these distractions.

Guide me to my self.

I release the old way.
I release the need to control.
I release the need to know.

I seek instead the experience
of Oneness.

Guide me in this.

October 4, 2008

51

Oil On Water

Old fears surface
like oil on water.

I no longer suppress their rising
for their intensity
thrives on inattention.

I welcome them.
They tell a story
of miscreation and
help guide me back
to truth
about myself
and those around me.

Their presence is a blessing.
For they tell me of my errors.

Not in deeds
but in thoughts.

Only peace exists.

Through our tortured thoughts
we hide our awareness
of peace.

Fear is the holy messenger that
tells us of our folly.

I now walk through the fear
and find
Peace.

April 14, 2009

The Journey

I have experienced the profound peace
of being connected to The Light.

I know the gentle presence
of Christ and his loving touch.

I know spiritual union with my brother.

I have experienced a state of being that is without limits
and without the singular sense of self.

I have experienced the answer to all the questions
that have been and will be posed throughout time.

I have learned that all questions are meaningless.

I know the joy of self love.

I have seen the veil of illusion that others extend
to hide their fears and I have glimpsed the glory
of their true selves.

I have talked with
mountains, rivers, waterfalls, trees, and animals
and they have shared their profound wisdom with me.

I know the voice of the Holy Spirit,
my Higher True Self.

I know the joy of the Holy Spirit working through me
to heal my thinking and that of my brothers and sisters.

I know and have experienced all these things
and now I seek
profound Joy.

I seek a full and boundless heart
Overflowing with Love.

I seek the full awareness of my creations
and the love that flows between us.

I seek the boundless joy of union
with my brothers and sisters.
and our Creator.

I know what I seek is already within me.
What I seek and am committed to is the full awareness
of this True State of Being.

As I ask, the answer is given:
I am Joy it is now time to live it.

August 20, 2012

Chapter III
True Sight

As we open our hearts to the awareness of our true self we begin to
see and experience others in deeper and more meaningful ways.
This seeing and experiencing is not from our five physical senses
but from a sixth sense. It is an inner True Sight and a knowing that
springs from a source of wisdom that is at the core of our spiritual
being. As such, it springs from Love and bathes everything in the
light of Truth. True Sight sees the pain and suffering of others but
knows it is a mere reflection of their fears and doubts. It sees past
the veil of self-deception to the true self. As with the foundations
to true self-awareness, True Sight needs to be nurtured and
exercised.

Many years ago I visited a spiritual community and found that the
matriarch of the community was both revered and feared. This
confused me. During a prayer circle I stood next to her and held
her hand. Early on my spiritual path I found that through physical
touch I could pick up on the energy of others. As I held her hand I
felt a layer of energy that I could only describe as the absence of
warmth. But beneath the cold I sensed very intense healing and
profoundly spiritual energy. I was confused by these seemingly
contradictory experiences and later went to that inner voice of
wisdom that I discussed earlier and asked for clarity. Three images
came forward, reeds in water, an oak tree, and the stars. I saw that
the reed represented the self that is immersed in the physical world
with all its responsibilities, contradictory emotions, and self-
doubts. The Oak represented her spiritual striving that was at its
core loving and nurturing. The stars were her spiritual self. This
experience led to the writing of the poem "The Reed" which is the
first of the poems in this chapter. I share this story as an example
of how we can nurture True Sight by not accepting the judgments
that come through our physical senses and analytical mind. By
opening our awareness to another way of seeing and experiencing
we can get a much richer and more meaningful understanding of
those around us.

When we connect to the truth of another we are in reality connecting to our truth. So as you experience these poems view them as messages to your self. While the poems were written with specific people in mind, their message is universal. We are all struggling with the same issues and at our core our striving is the same. We seek love and acceptance above all else. To see another truly is healing for it frees the other from the bonds of the false perceptions and judgments they hold against themselves. See yourself through the experience of these poems. Collectively they reflect back to you that which is your true self.

The Reed

You are the Reed,
You are the Oak,
You are the Stars.

The Reed is your earthly existence.
You are immersed in emotions
which sustain your physical form.

The Oak is your spiritual striving.
It is the self that shelters others
with love and compassion.
It is the self that reaches to The Light.
It is the self that is grounded
in the knowledge of your true Divinity.

The Stars are your spiritual self.
Your radiance is love.
You create through love and
and all that you turn your thoughts toward
is blessed.

June 2005

We See You

We see you.
You bring
Joy,
Love,
Innocence,
Acceptance
to those you touch.

You do not always see
these qualities in yourself.
But they spring from who you are.
We are your believing eyes.
We are blessed by
your gifts.

You are on a new path.
There is joy and uncertainty.
We rejoice in your joy
and support you
in your uncertainty.

We know you.
Our hearts are joined.
Our paths are different
but the same.
We each travel a
Path of the Heart.

When uncertainty is with you
go to your heart.
There you will find us.

We see you.
We Love You.
You are in our Hearts

May 20, 2006

The Veil

The veil is lifting.
Light is filling the darkness.

It is the dawning of a new way of being.
You sense this change
Self-doubt is diminishing.

The One you hesitate to name
walks with you.
Open your awareness
to this presence.

As the dawn of a new day
brings light where there was darkness,
let the guidance that surrounds and fills you
lead you to the Light that is your true self.

June 2, 2012

A Son's Prayer

I know your Heart.

It is pure and loving.
It is giving and desires nothing in return
but friendship.

Your Heart is playful.
To be with others in fun
makes your Heart sing
with delight.

Your Heart is sentimental
and sheds tears of deep joy
when it experiences the love of others.

I know your Heart
Because it is also my Heart.
I am your son. Our Hearts are one.

I know your Heart and
I Am Grateful.

I am your son and
I Am Grateful

My Heart sings with the
Love it holds for you.

February 2006

Nick's Song

You are a Child of the Light.
Others see what is hidden from you.
The brilliance of your Heart.

For now you live in the mind where
the shadow dwells.
This will change.
You are on a new path.
You are awakening from the shadow
into your true self.
Your Heart will be your guide.

You are a healer.
Not of the body but of
The Mind,
The Spirit,
The Earth.

Your instrument of healing is
Community.
You are of the People.

Your Truth lies in the Heart of the Community
for it is also your Heart.

Your path is not hidden from me
and I rejoice.
You will walk in joy.
You will know
who you are.

You are a Child of the Light.
You are my son and
this is my blessing.

March 8, 2006

Mathew's Song

You are my son.
You are a gift of God.
My joy in you started as a thought.
My joy in you truly manifested
when I first heard your heart
beating within your mother's womb.

I know your heart:
It is pure,
It is giving,
It is playful.

I know your heart
and it brings me joy.

The joy that is in your heart is
my blessing.

Follow your joy and you honor yourself.
Follow your joy and my heart sings.
Follow your joy.
You are a gift of God.

March 8, 2006

Michael's Song

I see you.
It is your Heart
that shines through.
I saw it in our first meeting.
I saw it during times of pain,
and times of joy.
Times of celebration
and times of sadness.

I see the strength and caring that you
freely give to others.
I see the compassion
that extends to those around you.
I see a friend;
I see a brother.

I feel you in my heart.
It is a love that runs
to the depth
of my being.
My Heart sings
with the joy
of our friendship.

As you have given
it is now your time for receiving.
This is your challenge.
See the love that surrounds you.
Giving is our blessing.

I see you.
It is your Heart
that shines through.

June 30, 2006

Carol's Song

You are the morning star.
Full of energy and
signaling the possibilities
of the coming day.

The warmth of your Heart
is easily felt as you
eagerly extend yourself to others.

Your subtle elegance
and grace of movement
reflect your spirit which seeks
the love of those close to you.

This is your time of receiving.
As you have sought love so too have you received.
But you have not always felt the love that is returned.
This is your challenge.

Be at peace.
I feel your warmth.
I know your caring heart.
I see the artist in all that you do.
I see the love that surrounds you.

I see you.
You signal the possibilities
of the coming day

July 1, 2006

Dream Catcher

Dream Catcher!
I see you.
I know you.
My eyes have been shut
but now they are open.

We have come a long way old friend.
The old ways have served us well,
but we are now on a new path.
You have led others to their dreams
and shown them their potential.

It is now time for you to pursue your dreams.
I do not see your path.
But Hawk has keen eyes.
Search your Heart for Hawk.
He will guide you.
He knows the path.

Oh! I do see something.
I see your stories.
There is power
and good medicine here.
Is this your path?

The answer has already
been given to you.

Dream Catcher.
I know you.
My eyes have been shut.
Now they are open.
My Heart is filled
with joy.

August 4, 2006

Song Bird

You sing from
your Heart.

The sounds are pure
and remind of us
of who we are.

You are the Song Bird.
You remember
the voice of our father.
It flows through you
like thundering
waters passing over a
a magnificent waterfall.
Yet the sound
that comes forth
is gentle
like a flowing brook
as it winds through
a garden forest.

This is your service
to others.

The Voice of God
flows through you
and reminds us
who we are:
The daughters
and sons
of God.

December 30, 2006

Illusion

You are surrounded by darkness.
As I go deeper I see Light.
It extends into infinity.

I feel the heaviness of your Heart.
It blocks the Light.

You believe you are not worthy.
So you keep yourself separate from your true self
and from others.

With a quiet mind and
without judgment
go to your Heart
and seek
the Pure Love
that is there.

Submerge yourself
in this Pure Emotion.
Become this feeling of Love.
Extend it inward.
Into what you know as yourself.
Feel the joy!
Feel the Love explode
as it expands
into infinity.

Know this as your true self.
You are surrounded by Light.

All else is illusion.

February 21, 2007

It Is The Light

The Day has come.
It is a time of rejoicing.
It is a time of healing.

As the Oak strives for the Light
so too have you.
Be not afraid for
Light surrounds you.

I see blue light.
It is the blue that fills
the cloudless afternoon sky.
It is a promise
that all is right
and nothing else exists

I feel the Love
that is within you.
It is calming.
It is ever present.
It is the Light.

May 27, 2007

Sky and Earth

One is Sky
the Other Earth.

One fills the Other;
with Light,
the promise of
the coming day,
and the mystery of
a cloudless night.

The Other is the ground
upon which dreams flourish
and spring to life.
The vessel from which
flow the nurturing waters
that calm and inspire
the spirit.

They have come together
Sky and Earth.
Their covenant is Joy.
Their purpose is Peace.
Their creative source
is Love.

June 12, 2007

Dragonfly

Like the wings
of the Dragonfly
Light shines through you
and is transformed
into a spectrum
of Divine colors.

Know that this requires
no need for action
on your part.
This is merely your nature.
Your Being creates
peace and beauty.

You struggle against this,
which brings you disharmony.
You believe that it is action
that will bring you happiness.
This is illusion.

Allow life to flow
from you and through you.
Make your choices in the moment.
From your Heart.
Trust in this.
Trust in your self.

Like the wings
of the Dragonfly
You bring magic and color
wherever you go.

July 11, 2008

Sarah and Matt

Sarah, I see the love that fills you.
It is a nurturing life force
that is at the base
of your creative self.

Your healing abilities spring
from this creative source.

It is your heart
that will lead you
in your life's work.

In time
it will lead you
in all relationships.

- - -

Matt you are the rock
upon which dreams are built.

You see others
as they are and
as they wish to be seen.

Above all
you see into their Hearts:
Their hopes,
their dreams,
and their doubts.

But it is the hopes and dreams
You respond to.

In this way
you bring healing
and purpose to others.

I also see the love
that flows between you both.
I sense the gentleness
and calm in your joining.

Know that it is this
that will sustain your relationship
and allow it to grow
and be a nurturing force
for you both.

May 13, 2010

The Golden Bridge

We see a golden bridge surrounded by Light.

We see two hands reaching out though the brilliance finding each
other.

We see the Love that fills you both.

We see the gratitude that you extend to each other.

We see the calm water that flows from your joining.

We see the rock upon which your relationship
will grow.

We see the Love that will define your path.

We are the believing eyes that rejoice in your journey.

We are the open arms that cradle your hopes
and dreams.

We are simply among the many that are blessed
by your love.

March 12, 2011

Chapter IV
The Other Side

Death is at the center of our fears for we have been taught and have come to believe that the essential quality of death is loss. We are taught that life ends at death and when another dies we lose any "real" connection with them. Sure their memory continues to live within us, but they are gone and for all intents and purposes, our relationship with them is gone and can no longer be experienced in any "true" sense.

As I progressed in my inspirational writing I began to experience the relationship between the living and the dead. One day I was talking with my sister-in-law about her father who had died some time ago. As she talked I could feel the love she still held for him and then I sensed that there was love being returned to her and I knew it was from her father. This was a totally new experience for me. Like my other intuitive awakenings there was absolutely no doubt to the authenticity of the experience. It simply felt natural and I knew that within this flow of love there were messages to be shared. Upon my returning home I sat down at my computer, brought into my awareness the flow of love I experienced and a poem from her father came forward. This is the first poem in this section.

Following this experience more poems came forward from loved ones who had passed and in a few cases children who were yet to be born. In each case I first felt a loving connection between the person on the "other side" and the friend or relative. Through these poems I was able to get a sense of the nature of life after physical death. What I experience from those who have passed is a sense of clarity and calm along with a non-judgmental awareness of the challenges that they still face and were left unresolved in their passing. Above all there was absolute clarity and gratitude of the love that was extended them in life and the love that continues to be shared even after the death of the physical body.

I Am With You.

I am with You.
I am the morning dew
sparkling with the vibrancy
of the rising sun.

I am the songbird
perched outside your kitchen window.

I am the gentle vibration
in a beautiful melody
first heard.

I am the love in your Heart
when your thoughts turn to
a dear friend.

I am the evening star
on a clear night
that calls to your imagination.

I am the warmth you feel
when you hold your
lover's hand.

I am your father.
My love is pure and shines
brighter than all the
suns of all
the galaxies.

I am your father.
I am with you.

April 17, 2006

To Be With You

I want to be free;
to live
to love
to be with you.

I know not my journey.

It is a journey of the Heart.

I am afraid.

Be not afraid,
I am with you now
I have always been with you.

My Heart is empty.
Ah, but I sense your presence
and I feel hope.

It is not our time of joining.
You have a path to walk for now.

You give me strength.
I will walk this path - for now.
I am content for I can feel your presence.
You are in my Heart.

Yes. Go to your Heart
and be not afraid.
I am with you now
and forever.

I am at peace.
You are in my Heart[1].

May 8, 2006

---

[1] This was written for a man who was in a hospital room near mine. I visited him several times but we were not able to talk because of his condition. My sense was that this poem came through me from a soul mate that had died.

I Am At Peace

I am at peace.
I have lived,
I have loved,
I have learned.

Your music is with me now.
It is the symbol of your essence.
It brings me great joy
as you have brought me joy.

Forgive me for at times fear and pain
have guided my physical life.
I am a child, but growing in the ways of
the Heart.
The ways of Spirit.

Follow your joy.
Your Heart is strong and pure.
It guides you well.

Be at peace.
I am at peace.
I know love.
I know you.
You are my son.
My blessing.

I am at peace.

May 10, 2006

I Am the Setting Sun

You are on a new path,
as I am.
Our lessons have been that of
Love and joy,
not pain and sorrow.

Follow your joy.
Only the joy is true.
Pain and sorrow
no longer serve you.

Your Heart is pure
as our love is pure.
I am the setting sun.
Rejoice in the day that was,
but find your joy
in each new day.

I am at peace.
I walk a new path.
It is a path of the Heart.
I feel your love.
It is my blessing.

We are one.
We are on our path of return.
Follow your joy.
There is where you will find me.

May 16, 2006

You Are In My Heart

You are in my Heart.
I am at peace.
You brought joy to my life.
I did not always show it.
My joy was tempered by past hurts
and worries about the future.

God is with you.
He is hidden from your awareness.
But not from mine any longer.

You have much love in your Heart.
Do not be afraid.
You are loved.
It is a love freely given.
It does not need to be earned
and it will never be withdrawn.
Trust in this
and follow your joy.

I am at peace.
You are in my Heart

July 6, 2006

A Birth Mother's Song

I am with you.
You are the perfect son.
You taught me
that my shame was an illusion.

That your presence in my life was
an act of love
and an awakening
to love.

Your love has always been with me,
as my love is with you now.

Your pain is my pain.
Your joy my joy.
You are worthy of only happiness.

Allow me to comfort you.
Allow me to hold you in my arms.
Allow me to tell you that I love you.
You are worthy of this and more.
Claim your joy
not your pain.

I am with you.
I have always been with you.
I am only one of many.
Allow our love.
We are timeless
as is our love.

September 14, 2006

Love Surrounds You

I see the tears
But what I experience
is the love
they conceal.

Be at peace.
Love has been my lesson.
Close your eyes
and feel the Love
that surrounds you.
I am with you as
you are with me.

We are one.
I dreamed of isolation
and unworthiness.

But you brought Love
and true companionship
into my awareness.
Through your eyes
I saw Truth.

The Love you have extended to me
is now my gift to you.

Learn from my example.
Awaken from the dream and
know that you are
a child of God
and most worthy of
the Love that surrounds you.

October 10, 2006

You Are My Blessing

I am at peace.
It is not the true peace of The Heart
for I am still new in such matters.

It is a contentment that is enough for now.

I have experienced Love.
It shines through you
onto me.

It's memory
is now a beacon
for me.
You are with me
and I with you.
This is a knowing
of the Heart.

You have been my teacher
and my blessing.
Do not doubt this.

I walk my path.
It has not been a path of peace.
But you and others have shown me
a new path:
The path of Love;
The path of forgiveness.
A path of
the Heart.

I am grateful.
You are my blessing.

December 26, 2006

The Beauty In My Heart

You are both the beauty
in my Heart.

You have been my joy.
Do not take fault
in my actions.

You are the expression of love
I could not shine upon myself.

I felt your love
and this helped sustain me.
But my path took a turn
not of your doing.

Love
is the only
true inheritance
I can give you.
I do so
with a Heart
that is at peace
and filled with the joy
you brought me.

I see you truly.
I see the purity
of your hearts.
The Light
Shines brightly
within you both.

Much joy awaits you.
Follow the joy
that is of the Heart
This is your path.

You are the beauty
in my Heart.

December 27, 2006

Mike & Jim

The shadows surround me.
But I am not afraid.
I feel your love.

I follow the Light of
your Love.
There I find The Pearl.
It is our meeting place
Brother.

Yes, I feel your Love as well.
You have guided me
To this place of peace
and wonder.

It is now our place
of meeting.

The Joy softens the tears
of our parting.

Yet my sadness runs deep.
We had much yet to do.
I will miss the comfort of
your companionship.

Our work together will continue
and my companionship is Eternal.

I know this.
Yet the tears come.

They are tears of Love
and they honor me.

Yes – they are
tears of Love.

I feel your peace
and it comforts me.

October 7, 2007

Grandmother

Love flowed from her
like rays of the early morning sun
pushing away the darkness of night.

The shadow of guilt and shame
hid the Love that surrounded
the one she watched over.

She spoke her silent message
of love, compassion,
and innocence.

Through the darkness
her message was heard,
her love felt,
and the seeds of peace
planted.

Her presence was confirmed
not by the five senses
but by a deep knowing.

A certainty that only
Love is real.

She is with you - always.
She is your guide,

You know her as
Grandmother.

2010

I Am

Love shines though
even in the darkness.
This has been my lesson.

I felt your radiance
from the moment
you were born.
Darkness may intrude
upon your awareness
but know
it is not you.

My life was filled by love
and this is the inheritance
I extend to you.

As you are
the extension of my love
Your daughter
is the extension of your love.
Be at peace.
I am with you both.

I am
the Light that encircles
both of you.

I am
the flower
whose beauty
draws your attention.

I am
the songbird
who serenades
your approach.

I am
yourself
and my love for you
is boundless.

May 29, 2008

Renewal

As the rainbow signals renewal,
so does my death.

My lessons were painful and difficult.
Death is my renewal.

You have come through pain into peace.

My journey to peace is longer yet.

You are a light that signals hope.

Hope is my redeemer.

October 3, 2011

Promise

This is not
the end
of our journey.
Rather it is merely
a beginning.

My love for you
is not diminished
in death.
It flows freely
from my True Heart
to yours.

The veil does not
separate us.
We are sisters
and our bond
transcends
the physical.

Do not try to make sense
of my actions.
They sprang from madness
and no satisfaction
can be found there.

I feel your pain
but know
I have not
abandoned you.

When you are ready
open your Heart
and let us continue
our exploration
of truth.

We will guide
each other.

This was and remains
our promise.

October 21, 2011

You Brought Me Peace

You brought me peace
not discontent.

I loved you
from the first moment.

The discontent I projected
came form a love
that was grounded in fear
not in judgment against you.

I feared your choices
would bring only pain.

I see now
that they lead you
to the loving women
you are now.

My error was thinking
I knew the course
for your happiness.

My love for you
is unshakable.

I see the
Grace that fills you.

You have been
and remain
my blessing.

July 7, 2014

Chapter V
Conversations with Spirit

When I am most troubled, confused, and in need of clarity, I write out a question then quiet my mind and let the answer come to me. There are other times when I would like a better understanding about an occurrence in the world, my life, or a particular spiritual concept and I will use this same technique to get answers.

While the source is the same as the poems these writings are much more interactive and conversational in nature. Even though the responses that come forth are often poetic in their simplicity and style, I do not write them as poems but as a dialogue. This chapter is dedicated to these wisdom writings.

July 25, 2006 - Are you with me? I feel discontent.

We are with you.
All is well.
Trust and live each moment in joy.
Forgive for nothing has truly happened.
You dream.
You can shape the dream for you are its maker.
You have learned how not to fear.
In subtle ways you still fear but you are learning.
Your intentions guide what is manifested.
We hear you and support your wishes.
Your path is our path.
We love you.
Perfection cannot be improved upon, only experienced.
When you join your awareness to the Creator you get a sense of your perfection.
Continue this practice.
When you are ready, pick up your studies in the Course[2].
Find your own study group.
We will guide you.

---

[2] A Course In Miracles

October 29, 2006 - Speak to me. I wish to hear your voice.

How is this?

It is fine. I wish to publish my poems. Will this serve our Father?

You serve Him now just as you are.

Will my poems help bring me and others out of the illusion. Is it in service of the Light?

Yes. They come from your heart. You have opened up yourself to our voice and others will see this in your poems.

You fear.

Yes. But I know this is just part of my wrong mind. I am tired in many ways.

That is because you try to control. Pursue what brings you joy.

I enjoy creating things that will help others.

We will guide you. Take a step at a time and we will provide the stepping stones.

OK. Thank you. I am grateful.

We know and we love you.

January 1, 2007 - What is the meaning of what just happened? (I was writing an intuitive poem and the words stopped coming – this has never happened before and it disturbed me).

It is nothing.

You live in a dream – some things are meant to distract you from your path –your true self.

You are learning to live truth but at times the illusion prevails – this is your distraction –your dream – nothing more.

You can not lose us and the wisdom that has always been yours.

We are here to remind you and to show you where it lies.

You speak from your heart as you write from your heart. This is your gift.

Be at peace and know us as the Love that rests in your Heart.

We know your gratitude and while this is good, it is not lost because your words appear to have disappeared. We do not read your words but we do know what is in your heart for it is also our heart. We are one with you. And yes our path is your path. We return as One as we left as One.

February 10, 2007 - Are you with me now?

You know I am.

Why do I feel so distant from your voice at times?

You are learning to open your heart anew. You seek the truth which you do not understand. You know where it lies and as you get closer you doubt. This is the way of the ego. But do not be harsh for this is the path of return.

Your experiences are new and you yearn for the old. The old brought you to this place but it no longer serves you. In this, follow the teachings of Abraham. It is through your preferences that you will find your way.

You seek the calm waters of the Holy Spirit. Your preferences will guide you. Serve yourself as you serve others. Be at peace. We are with you and you know us. We cannot fail you for we are one and we know the way.

I seek union with God – I seek union with my brothers and sisters.

Find union with yourself. Seek the calm waters that are within you. We will guide you.

Was my dream last night of extending Love your teaching?

Yes,

Why was it also disturbing?

You seek perfection within the physical – this is the trick of the ego. Seek joy and do not judge the joy.

I believe I understand. Extending love to myself is joyful. But as I think on this I feel discomfort – I miss my brothers and sisters.

We know. This is your purity of spirit – allow your inward journey to encompass your brothers and sisters. They are always with you.

Yes that feels right – thank you..

You know your doubts only serve distraction. You need not fight them for it only makes them seem real. It is only the power that you give them that brings discomfort.

Continue with the Course In Miracles lessons. They bring you peace. The time of delay is over – you are on the right track with your new practice.

Yes I feel this truth in my heart. The lessons do bring me peace.

Why do I fight it so?

You still believe in time and use this to manage the illusion. The lessons are not a management tool for time or the illusion. They lead you out of the illusion.

Do not judge yourself through what I have said. You have decided for the Holy Spirit and all that you do is not in vain.

Thank you for your guidance and presence in my life.

We are one.

March 22, 2007 - I seem to be off-balance – my mind and feelings are so changeable. It is like I do not have a foundation or grounding. What is wrong? What do I need to do to find peace?

It is a time of change. You question everything and this creates confusion. Trust in the process – be at peace with wherever you are in the physical and emotional. Be the observer without judgment. Note that you are not at peace but do not judge – you are where you need to be, learning what you need to learn.

Your ego is strong and wishes to regain control – it has questions but no answers – you are always able to find the answer eventually and usually sooner rather than later. Your Heart does tell you when you are on the path of truth – continue to develop your heart.

Be at peace - we will guide you. Our love is eternal and our path is with you.

I am grateful.

We feel and know your love.

March 25, 2007 - How are the level of form and the level of Spirit related?

They are not related in any true sense for one is real and the other is illusion. On the level of form their relationship is simple. Within your mind – not your brain- you know who you are and that this world of the physical in no way defines you. It is the part of your mind which you call Spirit or Your Higher Self or Christ which seeks your conscious awareness and with your permission can shape your physical experiences in such a way to help teach and lead you to your true nature.

So how do I tell this to others in my book?

They are concerned with happiness in the physical – until you can demonstrate (as you have with your students) that this spiritual striving brings peace and joy on the level of the physical, they will continue to look elsewhere. This is in part a deception for it could be used to keep them stuck in the illusion. But we have taught you the cost that eventually comes when you fail to progress along the spiritual path. Teach this as well.

What do you mean by *"This is in part a deception"*?

Spiritual striving is at its core the process of changing your mind about the nature of yourself and the world that seems to surround you. As you proceed along this path peace and happiness becomes increasingly the foundation of your inner experience. But there are still lessons to learn and false self judgments to heal. Thus discontent (anger, fear, anxiety, etc.) is also experienced. This is necessary for discontent becomes the motivator for change or put another way a signal that your thinking is in need of healing.

The deception is that some students may see the absence of peace as a failure on their part rather then a signal that they have judged against them selves. In such cases their primary investment is in maintaining peace rather then healing their mind.

Guide me – I feel your love.

We are with you – this is also our path. You know this.

Yes.

We will guide you.

Is there a "but"?

Yes and no: You set limits on your striving that we honor.

What are the limits I set?

You are afraid of failure so you move with caution and hesitation.

I know – how do I move through this – this is my desire.

Set time for this as you have started. As you focus your energy so do you focus your intention.

What about my many projects?

Do not worry about how your projects will manifest – leave that to us.

May 7, 2007 - Darkness surrounds me. I am confused. The old ways do not work as well. But I can still find your presence – it is always there. But it is harder to hear Your voice. Your guidance.

I am with you.
My voice is still strong and you hear it but your trust has been shaken.

I am confused by the words of others. I no longer trust what I experience. I know that I need to move to a deeper understanding of your presence. But the transition is a difficult one.

You need not try so hard. Where you are and where you want to be are closer than you think. Trust in your path and in my guidance.

What of my physical concerns? What is the answer to their resolution?

They are tied to your wanting. Be at peace with yourself. The rest will take care of itself.

What of my striving? My desire to serve?

You serve now as you always have. You are a great teacher – this is the purpose you chose. You need not mistrust this path. It will unfold as it should.

You hurt and you fear emptiness,
But you also feel the presence of our connection.

Yes it is this awareness that sustains me and is my beacon.

Why does the emotional clearing
seem to not be as powerful a tool as it once was?.

You have cleared much of the fear that has surrounded your awareness.
What is left is old patterns of thinking.
Your ego struggles for control and
has become more aggressive.

You feel drawn more to meditation.
To quieting your mind.
Pursue this path.

May 16, 2007 - My mind is cluttered and my emotions dark. What is happening to me? The guidance I receive is affirming yet I do not feel at peace. The things I have learned are now brought into question. I am holding onto something that needs to be let go. The things that torment me:

- Am I serving my purpose? The things I would write about no longer seem to work for me. Are they a lie?

102

No they are part of Truth as you know it and they still serve you.

- My emotions are so variable. Emotional clearing does not seem to work as the emotion returns. It seems I am growing further from my Heart and the peace I have felt.

I feel that you have forsaken me. It is harder to sense your presence. There is part of me, a knowing that is aware of this falsehood. A knowing that you are with me, as you have always been. But it is difficult to feel your presence.

I am with you as I have always been. You doubt and this separates us. Be at peace as this will pass. I do communicate with you in different ways through your brothers and sisters. You have detected a quality in your giving that does not serve you – a need to help that you believe defines you. This thought is limiting for nothing defines you except Love. No service or action is a worthy description of your being. You have opened yourself to service and I will use you. You have asked that what you do be in your highest good and that of your brother – in this I guide you. Do not fear for your intentions are pure – while your actions may be contaminate, it is your intention that people sense and respond to. You judge yourself harshly.

Your tools still work but you are learning to use them in a more refined way. Allow the process to unfold. New lessons are coming your way and with them clarity.

May 22, 2007 - I am not my body

This morning as I was meditating I felt a dull pain in my chest – it is a familiar pain and one that comes at times when I try to quiet my mind or focus on my Heart Center. As I went into the pain, the image of someone stabbing me repeatedly with a spire came to me. It seemed to be a past life memory. My first instinct was to get him to stop the stabbing. But what I actually did was draw my awareness away from the body – with this came the realization that I was not the body being abused. Nor did I feel compelled to stop the person stabbing the body but rather said to him something like, "This body must have wronged you." It was a statement of understanding not judgment. By this time the pain was gone. The lesson seems clear – all attack is of no consequence. It needs no response or judgment for it is not being done to me – it represents the torment of the other and this only needs be addressed through understanding and compassion.

July 11, 2008 - Tell me about forgiveness.

"Forgiveness is the extension of Love. There may be the perception that some action seemingly directed at you was done in anger or some other disquieting emotion. But there is a deeper awareness of the divine nature of the other and the total discontinuity of the others' actions. Thus your response is to the truth of who the other person is, not to the false image they hold up of themselves. This false image is merely ignored – it does not exist but in the mind of the other. Thus the natural response is Love – which essentially shatters the illusion and restores the other to their natural state."

August 6, 2008 - How do I wake up?

You ignore the dream's seeming effects. They are not real. They are just made-up emotions and frustrations. You need neither push them away nor dwell on them. They are like a mirage. You can look upon them and see how they resemble the physical world but you know it is only a reflection. You can perceive the beauty in this or the crudeness of the distortion. Love extends love. Thus love only sees the true image that the mirage reflects and not the reflection. This is what the Course calls true perception.

Your feelings other than true love are but judgments against your self that make the dream seem real. Free yourself through recognizing the error you make.

Love surrounds me and what I perceive with my five senses is but a distortion of Truth. My error is in simply believing my five senses rather than my true heart, which tells me Love is with me always. Within the dream I have made an error and listened to my ego. I no longer choose to listen to the ego but rather my true self – The Christ within. My error is thinking the mirage is real. It is a simple mistake which I forgive and wish to correct at all times in the moment. Guide me in this.

October 3, 2007 - A Journey with Michael[3],

I have traveled to the center of the Universe and touched The Mind of God. A brother took me. It was not a place nor was it an experience defined in any way by our five senses of sight, sound, touch, smell or taste. There was no he or I. There was no us. There was no thought. It was simply The State of Being. There was perfect peace, perfect love, and boundless clarity. We embarked on this journey with a question, "Am I worthy"? In that instant of Perfect Being every question I had ever asked or ever will and every doubt that had ever crossed my mind was answered. All my questions, doubts and fears were not real. They were all part of a dream and having awakened from the dream to my true self they no longer had any meaning whatsoever.

January 30, 2009 - Conversation with Christ

Thank you for your presence in my life.

We are blessed as one.

Am I close to the end of this journey to the awareness of my Spirit and our Oneness?

---

[3] I sat with a friend almost every day over the course of a year. He had lung cancer and one week before he died we shared this experience which is from my journal.

Yes you are close.

I feel that I can reach out and touch you.
Feel the gentle coarseness of your robe.
The fullness of your hand.
Are these things my ego struggling to stay in the illusion?

No, it is the movement of Love outward from your Heart to My Heart which are one.

Be at peace and allow your true self to emerge as it will on it's own.
There is nothing you need to doubt. Surrender to the love that is within and without.

Thank You for your Presence.

I am at peace.

April 24, 2009 - Tell me about compassion.

"Compassion is the extension of love".

How is compassion different from Love?

"Love simply Is. Compassion only exists within the physical world".

As I wrote, the notion of a parent and a small child came to me. The following came to me neither as a story nor as a description of something I witnessed unfolding within my inner vision. Rather what I received was an experience with the sense of knowing. It is difficult to convey the wonder of such an experience even though I have experienced this many times. It is not "thought" in the sense that we think with our minds. It is simply a knowing. It is an experience of great love with a message that is revealed as a whole at once. However, I am unable to convey the message as a whole but rather must break it down and use words that were in reality

106

not part of the experience. What I write will be in a story format but know it did not come to me this way - it is the only way I can think of to share the learning that came through the experience.

The child had done something that some, including the child, might have thought of as a misdeed. However, the parent only saw the purity that is the child and did not focus even for an instant on the "misdeed" but on the truth of who this child is. I could feel the immense Love that flowed from the parent to the child and I did experience the parent's experience of the child as a being of Pure Light. The parent was aware that the child had made misjudgment against himself and in so doing had lost sight of who he really was. The parent saw this error but the Love and Truth of who the child is never escaped the parent who saw things truly. The parent was totally grounded in "Truth" – never lost sight of who the child is and could see the error but was not disturbed by this.

From this perspective (Compassion) the parent could correct the child's error. And it is from this perspective that we best correct our own errors.

The nature of compassion:

- *Compassion is an extension of Love within the physical world.*
- *Compassion completely overlooks what might be considered mis-action/misdeeds (behavior) in self and others.*
- *Compassion comes from the recognition that the self or another has made a negative misjudgment about themselves. Thus Compassion is the correction of error - in thought.*
- *Compassion is centered in the "Knowledge" of the divinity of the self and others.*

August 19, 2009 - I feel your presence. It is subtle yet not.

*You have attuned yourself to our vibration. This is real. We are
your self.*

*Know that what you experience including our voice is the voice of
your Higher Self, the Voice of God, for it springs from your love as
you spring from God's Love.*

*Nothing is wasted in the dream. (It springs from the truth of who
you are as it also does from that part of you which hides in the
dream)?. One is real the other is not. Which do you think speaks
the loudest? Not in volume but in the truth of knowing?*

*Love is all that matters in the dream. All else is distraction. There
is no right relationship or wrong relationship. All leads you to
Love.*

What about my book? I seem stuck.

*The book will come in time when you are ready and it serves
your's and Love's purpose which is one in the same.*

*Your discontent is of your making and no one else's. Your ego
desires fame and fortune but you fight against the responsibility.
This is good as you are searching for your true heart's desire. You
wish to be of service and this is good as well. You sense the love
that you are and the strong desire to extend the love. But you feel
limited. Do not focus on the product but rather the experience.
Each experience is a guide to your healing and your path of
awareness. Nothing is lost or lacks a purpose that is not of God,
for it comes from you. Even though it is a dream, your Love always
prevails as it is the stronger force even in the dream where only
opposites can seem to be. Know that you are the Son of God. This
awareness will always be. You Are as God Is. You lose nothing,
only discontent as you awaken. Follow the guides that surround
you and lead the way. They have awakened as you have as well.
They are aware and you are not.*

Thank You for your love and guidance.

*We serve you.
We are your self.*

September 16, 2009 - I feel blocked

Go to your heart.

It is hard. The pain and distraction are so very strong. It is a very old experience that has been absent for a long time. Is it my vanity at work?

Yes.

It feels less now.

Allow what is your experience within the illusion but know that you are love and nothing else. All discontent is illusion.

I wish to help bring about change within this world and within those in pain.

This is your function. Opportunities for healing will come to you naturally. This you need not control.

What is it that is at the base of the discontent?

Fear of course. Fear that you are making wrong decisions and taking wrong actions. Fear that you are fooling yourself. Love is strong in you and you cannot stray far from your path. You have opened yourself to guidance and cannot fail.

What is my lesson from this experience?

That your worldly heart may guide you to false idols but your true heart will prevail. Do not fret for even actions from your worldly heart cannot do harm.

What is my worldly heart?

This is part of the ego self that believes it is in service to the Heart. It is the part of you that wants "'right action" but it is really just the ego masquerading as Wisdom. This leads to misdirected action. Left unchecked, this aspect of your ego self leads to vanity and pride, meaning actions that are ego-inflating as opposed to Spirit-supporting.

Thank you. I do feel better.

We are blessed to serve.

September 25, 2009 - Tell me about our spiritual heart.

Deeds are not of men but of their hearts.
There is but one heart and but one deed,
Which is the extension of Love.

The Heart has no gender and no other purpose.
Within the physical it extends itself through the eyes of the perceiver.

When the fragmented self opens itself to love it sees love's reflection within the world. When the self closes itself to love it sees fear's reflection within the world.

We open ourselves to love's presence by the inward search for peace. Peace is of God's making and discontent is of our making. Peace is not something we must earn. It simply is. We can only open or close our awareness to peace.

February 4, 2010 - Discontent seems to fill me. I am present with it but it is wearing. I feel Love well up in me as my thoughts turn to your voice. What am I to do?

Follow our guidance. It is the resonance in your Heart. You seek fame and fortune but know this is not a sure path to peace. Allow what will be and what will come.

We have started pebbles rolling through your action and each pebble loosens two each of which looseness two and so on. What has started cannot be stopped. Even your discontent will not slow the avalanche. You have set your heart on an irrevocable course and you know this. Be at peace. Your choice has been made and we have responded to your call. No force can stop us, even your discontent.

I follow the path now of self-love. Is this a worthy path?

It is the only path. You have opened your self to the love that surrounds you. Now open yourself to the Love that fills you.

It is hard and I know doubt.

Ah, but you know the experience of Love.
It is like the most powerful magnet in your world and you are but a pebble of steel.
It pulls you and the shear power of its attraction exhilarates you. The force of its attraction compels you. You are the magnet and the pebble of steel. You are being drawn to your Self. To wholeness, to completion, to Creation, to Love.

Emotional clearing is a tool. You use it every day and almost every moment. It serves you as it serves others. You are digging deeper and deeper into your subconscious. You think you are mining lead but you are mining the materials from which you will make Gold. This is your alchemy. Share the Gold through the teaching.

June 21, 2010 - Why do I feel such discontent?

We are with you. All is as it should be. You seek brothers and sisters in your quest for your role as helper and teacher. This is as it should be. We guide all that you do. You question your path and your choices. You follow what feels right in the moment and

111

this too is as it should be. Do not despair all will come into the Light. The time of doubting is coming to an end. Have faith.

November 10, 2010 - What is Fear?

Fear is the relinquishment of peace.
Peace is your natural state.
Fear arises when a thought that is not of God arises into your awareness.
The awareness can be conscious or subconscious.
The thought is often one of unworthiness.
You are of God and unworthiness is unknown to your Creator.
Thus fear is something you have made up.
As a child you try to make sense of your physical world.
Often the lessons of the physical world teach a child that they are flawed and must seek peace outside of them self.
Since peace is internal the seeking is without finding. In this way you come to believe that you are not worthy.
As the child grows up he or she projects unworthiness onto others. This is often done by viewing others as flawed.
To the extent that anyone views another as flawed, it reinforces the notion that they are flawed.
Neither perspective is true.
Fear naturally arises from this profound misconception.

Within the physical world, fear is pervasive. It is the natural consequence of the dualistic nature of the world you live in.
Within the realm of Spirit, Peace is pervasive. In this context the terms Love and Peace are interchangeable. Peace is the natural consequence of Oneness.

So how do I teach others to deal with duality in a way that will keep them centered in Peace?

Teach them about the nature of the world they live in, not through the "story" but through how they experience the world. Then guide them to their inner-wisdom to see the "story" from a place of Peace.

112

All paths to God are essentially the process of redefining the experiences of the physical world from one of misperception (fear/anger) to one of true perception (Peace/Love). There are no exceptions.

In teaching others, you must honor their experiences of both fear and peace. One tells them they are misperceiving and the other shows them the rewards for true perception. Perception changed from fear to Peace is irrevocable in that the karma which sets the stage for the lesson dissolves into nothing. Know that within this context karma is merely a "force within"[4] that leads us to the lessons we are to learn on our path to Peace.

Spirit guides each individual to the experiences they need on their journey to Peace. Each path is unique and will require unique skills and tools. Thus intuitive teaching focuses on what is being experienced. Essentially this will lead to "self-directed" learning. As a teacher your responsibility is to take the person's experiences and weave them into lessons both on essential intuitive tools for living within the physical world and tools for keeping themselves grounded in their true Spiritual self.

December 11, 2010 - I know this world is both a classroom and a distraction. Please explain further.

"Yes, you are in Heaven and yes you have obscured your vision and what you now see is like a mirage. Nothing occurs outside of Heaven. All that you experience is done so within Heaven."

How is God perfect and unchangeable yet He continues to expand? How does my experience with Michael (see October 3, 2007 - A Journey with Michael) relate to Heaven?

---

[4] What is a "Force within?" *It is discontent that you have given me to correct. Within this context you have formed a contract with me to teach and you have agreed to be the student. Thus it is simply a learning agreement between us.*

"You experienced true knowledge which is an aspect of Heaven. There is more. There is a creative aspect. True creation is not an act of completion or development, it is an extension of the Love force which is a part of God's nature. Breathing is part of your nature in this physical world but it does not change who you are in a physical sense. It sustains who you are. Love and the extension of Love is the essential nature of God. You think of creation as making something new – something different from yourself. This is a false notion. Creation is the extension of self."

In true creation is the expanded self exactly the same as the original Self?

"Yes. But you think on the level of form. There is no form in Heaven. There is only thought which is not the thought you think of but is closer to what you call experience. True knowledge is complete and thought as you practice it is not necessary. You know of what I speak for you have experienced this with Michael. Creation or the Extension of love is the same but a much deeper and more profound experience. Heaven has no form and the experience is something far beyond what you have experienced thus far. But the door has been opened and you get glimpses of what lies beyond."

"You have taken aspects of creation and produced representations in the physical world. A flower is such a representation. The true essence of a flower is not in its physical form but in the experience when it is first beheld. It is a moment of remembering. As you have learned, "studying" beauty is an aspect of the physical mind and thus cuts you off from the original experience. Studying beauty often leads to false idols. It is an attempt to recapture the original experience. But the looking is in the physical mind and can not be found. In this way art becomes an obsession. There are those who paint from the experience and thus come closest to true creation. They are teachers of the Heart."

February 10 2011 - Are you really there?

114

Yes.

I can feel you but I doubt.

We teach new ways of understanding and this is confusing to you.

What are the new ways?

You have learned much about your process. This has been freeing but can also be limiting. It is time for you to learn new processes – of conceptualizing how your connection to Spirit works. There are no limits and process can give the illusion of limits. We will teach you.

Thank you.

We love you.

I know.

August 21, 2011 – The dream world

From time to time I have dreams that are lessons in the nature of the physical world we live in. In this dream I am playing pinochle and am in the process of ordering my cards and figuring out a strategy for playing the hand. The person to my right leads the first card. In that instant more cards appear in my hand. Since I am to be the next person to play a card, I am furiously trying to order my cards again and figure out my play. Then more cards appear in my hand but they have flowers on them rather than numbers or face cards. Now I am totally confused about how to play my hand. The person to my left is becoming increasingly angry at my delays. I can tell that he is regretting my presence in the game and is verbalizing that my status as a player in the game is in jeopardy. He insists that I need to figure out what I did wrong if I am to continue. My partner, who is sitting across from me, is a very caring person and is consoling about my problems. In a caring tone she encourages me to figure out what I did wrong. Hard as I might, I cannot figure out what I did wrong. Suddenly the insight comes to me that if I have done nothing wrong I must be dreaming and in that instant I woke up from the dream.

The lessons I took out of this experience are:

- We often conduct our lives believing that there are rules which we must abide by to assure our status as a "player." However, life is always throwing us curves and changing the nature of the "game." We come to believe that these changes are somehow caused by our own actions and it is up to us to figure out our problem and correct it. However, the problem is not in our actions or lack thereof, but rather in our willingness to give as well as accept guilt.
- In the dream, both the "mean" character (Player to my left) and the "nice" character (my partner) had the same message. "You need to figure out what you did wrong". The fact is there was no wrong. "Shit happens" in this world we seem to inhabit and it has nothing to do with our actions or inactions. We always deal with what arises in the best way we can at the time. There are no exceptions to this.

2011 Unknown month - Is it ethical and safe to use intuition to get clarity about another person and their actions towards you without first directly asking their permission?

You are a six-sensory-being. It is not possible for you to not know these things. It is perhaps better to ask, "Is it ethical to remove the blocks to my intuitive awareness?" Put another way, "Do I deny my true nature in order to perpetuate a false story about myself and another?"

Put in this way you experience the humor in asking such questions.

But there is guidance we can give you. You wish clarity about another's actions towards you. There is an implied permission as the other person clearly has a contract with you. The contract is always around seeking love of self and the other. This is the true purpose of all relationships and any intuitive endeavor. Start your inquiry from your Heart Center (your highest vibrational state – a place of love) with the intention of finding understanding and clarity.

The true purpose of all intuitive endeavors is love of self and others.

2011 Unknown month - Tell me about praise and gratitude.

True praise is the full expression of Love from a Heart that is fully open. Gratitude is an expression of a heart as it is opening but has yet to experience Love in its fullness. Gratitude inevitably leads to praise.

December 5, 2011 - What wisdom do you have for me?

Be at peace. All is as it should be. You feel the love that flows between us. This is truth. Get out of your head – your judgments. You need not second-guess if this is of the ego. You feel your love for Glenda – This is Truth.

Yes I feel the love. This is the place I wish to stay.

You are in the place you desire already. Know this and living it will follow. Read Ken's words; there is wisdom and compassion - compassion for yourself. Your students need these reminders as well. They judge themselves harshly but they also know the love that surrounds them. You are their believing eyes. We are in control not your solitary self.

You sense meditation is a path for you. Yes and no. It is a step towards peace but it is not a central theme. Fear not your path is not as the reclusive monk. You have experienced this and know your passion is in relationship. This is your passion.

117

2012 Month Unknown - Tell me about the tiny mad idea.

The son of God knows his true self and resides with his father in perfection. The tiny mad idea grew out of love and the desire to extend itself. At the instant it was thought it was abandoned in amusement. An aspect of God's son was trapped for that instant in time. This is where your awareness lingers. You feel the love that envelops you even in time. You laugh because you know to separate from God is not real and not even remotely possible. It is an illusion. When you make it real you allow time to continue. When you no longer make it real time will end.

May 18, 2012 - What types of agenda items would it be most productive for group members to bring to our meetings?

"There are always fears associated with the channel to Spirit and as a result blocks are put up that must be removed to more consciously access the wisdom that is available to everyone. Thus one of the primary purposes of the group is to help remove these blocks.

However to focus exclusively on blocks is counter- productive because it can reinforce that blocks are real rather than a choice. It is important to also focus on the experience of being connected to the source of inner wisdom. This includes the synchronicities that occur on a daily basis, the connections/experiences you have which open your heart and the wonders that fill your life. By tuning in to these experiences you expand your awareness of the very real connection you have at all times with Spirit.

Help your students sharpen their awareness of both the fear experiences that block them from their intuition and the experiences which open their hearts and reinforces the connection they have to everything. Have them bring to group both experiences and the questions that arise out of these experiences."

June 12, 2012 - What is the nature of sin?

Sin is the perceived loss of Love. It is the belief that someone can be without Love.
Sin is a construct of the ego and does not exist outside the ego. The notion that love can be lost through deeds or thoughts is a means by which the ego reinforces the belief that you can be unworthy of God's Love. This is such a profound misconception that it literally makes an imaginary world that is unknown to God. God made his sons and daughters like himself through the extension of Love. Thus Love is inherent in his creations. God's perfection insures that the concept of lost love or sin is impossible.

2012 Month unknown - I wish to understand about how each generation affects the next and how to end discontent that goes across generations.

Every generation seeks to correct the mistakes that were made upon them. These efforts are motivated by love but most often they are brought forward from a place of fear. You have seen the love behind your parent's actions that at the time brought you discontent. You know their error was not in caring but in yielding to fear. This is the error that you rightly seek to correct. Teach this as part of your curriculum.

Year and month unknown - I wish to know more about this notion of multiple dimensions and how we move between dimensions.

"The ego is the source of the physical world. It has established many dimensions (alternative paths) all designed to keep you separated from Source awareness. As you proceed through a dimension you make choices based on the learning in the dimension you are in. With these choices you either stay on the original track established at incarnation or you switch to a new dimension based on the learning and decision you make. When the

choice you make reflects a movement towards Love and forgiveness you move to a dimension (lifeline) that is more influenced by your Higher Self as apposed to your ego self. In this case the life lines that you were formally on are no longer extended as a dimension because they no longer have a purpose either for the ego or your Higher Self. In essence you have come to recognize the falsity of those dimensions and in so doing they are undone".

August 22, 2012 - I sense a heart that is overflowing with Love. I experience calmness and a certainty that what I seek is manifesting. My thinking mind wants to interfere, but it is easily set aside.

"All this is true and we rejoice. You are coming into your true power. The illusion is losing its hold on your attention. Your passion is turning inward rather than outward. You sense the beauty, the love that is in everything you perceive. There is so little work yet to be done. Your thinking is becoming self-correcting in the sense that you have opened yourself to guidance from the Holy Spirit".

"You sense the true magic that is at your core and that of all that surrounds you. You have learned that the path to Being is a choice to live the experience of Being. To live Joy and Peace. It is not a striving it is a choice to be what you seek."

"Distractions will continue to fade. Nothing can stop you for the choice has been made and is being fulfilled."

"Yes we are with you and will continue to provide affirmation. But more and more you sense our presence and your true self. Affirmation is becoming a constant experience and no longer an occasional event. This is as it should be. You know Truth and are living it to a greater and greater extent. This will continue to grow in your awareness."

"Faith is your shield and protector. It is the rock on which your transformation is taking place. It is an irrevocable aspect of your being that will take you through all challenges to your awareness".

I am grateful.

September 28, 2012 - Tell me more about projection and awareness of Love's presence.

In so many ways you distract yourself through unnecessary thoughts. These can be subtle or overt projections you make about the world around you and yourself. You are learning that even seemingly innocent (minor) projections such as anticipating aspects of you day (either good or bad), day dreaming about what should be or what was, or what will be, even longing for a loved one are all distractions from the moment. You lose awareness of what is.

As you are discovering, the moment always contains love and wonder. You access it not through your five senses but through opening your heart (your imagination) to love's presence. In this context love and wonder are one. You are also learning that this experience is not a cognitive process but an experiential one. You actually feel and see through your mind's eye the Love that emanates from all things. There are no exceptions to the presence of Love in all things. Remember this is a dualistic world. Love and fear are the only true forces that exist in this world you have made. Love is based in truth and fear in illusion.

How do I stay grounded in this new awareness?

The process has begun within you and it cannot be stopped. You have glimpsed Truth and the ego's games are being revealed to you. You are becoming naturally vigilant to distraction. Simply allow this process to continue. Attune your self to the loving energy. It draws you and is becoming part of your passion simply because it feels better than distraction.

121

Thank you this has helped. I am grateful.

Our joy is in serving you.

October 15, 2012 - I feel sad this morning but I still sense you in my heart. Christ is within me as is the Mother. Where does the sadness come from?

You have touched the memory of the Love of God. This sadness goes to the core of the dream. It is an awakening that guides you as I guide you. You have noticed how the meanings of my words are taking on new and deeper meaning for you and the peace this brings you. Your experience of life is coming into balance and you sense the joy that is emerging. Stay the course. You are guided.

January 25, 2013 – Love Flows. Tell me more about this experience.

As you are experiencing, Love flows from and between everything within the physical world. There is no place, even in the dream, where love is not. This you are realizing. It is the key to the joy you seek. Nothing apart from Love can bring joy. There are no exceptions.

What about the joy we feel when we win at something.

Yes this is the joy of the ego. It is winning at the expense of another's losing. But implied in winning is that eventually you must lose. Then all the winning is for naught. Thus joy of the ego is not only temporary it is simply the apparent absence of discontent. It is not true joy, for true joy comes through joining. Winning reinforces the belief that we are separate and that only a few can win.

Continue to open yourself to the flow of Love. This is your purpose. You are doing well. We rejoice in your experiences.

122

This flow of Love does reflect a state of being that is your true self. This is why there is great wisdom and always clarity when your awareness moves to this flow. All is known and questions are meaningless.

Your book is an instrument for this awareness and it will guide others. As you are beginning to sense the writing is not about the words but rather the experiences that they elicit. Continue to reinforce this notion to the reader. The place for contemplation is not on the words but the experience of the words.

Spring 2113 - "What does it mean to be authentic from a spiritual perspective"?

"Authenticity represents a heart centered process (Spirit based) of discovering your true heart's desire (what is in your highest and best good) in any situation and advocating for your desire from a position of compassion and love.

It is also a process of looking through and past discontent to what is sought for not what is to be avoided. When you come upon a very ugly person the ego's response is to focus on the ugliness and to blame the person for being ugly or blame the self for holding such thoughts. But from a heart-centered approach it is a process of accepting your reactions and judgments and noting how they close or open your heart. From this perspective you can then make a choice to question your judgments and either seek an alternative perspective that is heart-opening or accept your judgments and proceed with acting on them. As you can see it is facing discontent from a position of self-responsibility. You are in control of your thinking (what you hold as true and what you hold as false) and the behavior that will spring from this thinking. In this way you come to recognize that discontent comes from within and not from without. While there may be external contingencies that trigger the discontent, they are in no way the cause. The true cause is always centered in false beliefs about the self. To accept responsibility from the position of correcting error in belief rather then placing blame on any form is at the heart of true authenticity".

August 12, 2013 - I am very confused about who I am in this instant

Am I the watcher, the decision maker? I have had experiences of me without a body as well as joining (Holy Instant) without a sense of me or the other - just oneness. But until now I realize that I have not fully accepted my self as Spirit. On many levels I believe that I am spirit but through all these marvelous experiences of Spirit I have kept a significant part of me separate as a watcher.

You do have a sense of a deeper self that is without form with a sense of complete joining and complete wisdom (God). You are still the watcher, the decision maker, the mind that believes itself separate from God. But you have decided for Love. It is a commitment that you feel deep within what you call your Heart which is simply your memory of Truth - of God - your True Self.

What "me" has decided?

The question is confusing for you because you still think in terms of levels. The self you now experience as you write, the self that is watching yourself as you write, the self that is totally at peace and lies in the background as you write, and the self that is talking to you through these words. There is only two in the dream, the ego and your Holy Self. The fear and thus your ego is strong but your Holy Self is stronger. You opened yourself to another way of experiencing things when at 19 you prayed and asked for help. In the truest sense this was an act of surrender in that you had no idea of the way to peace and thus surrender control (ego will). As you opened yourself to help from within a shift away from the ego to your true self as Spirit began. It is the disintegration of the ego and the emerging of your true self. The decision seems to be made by your separated self but it is actually your true self (God) reaching through the dream which you "thinned" through your asking (surrender). The asking in this way is important, as is

124

*knowing that you are asking yourself (your Holy Self) not
something outside of yourself. By asking you evoke your will and
what you ask for is in your power to receive. Remember you are
the Son of God and your power is that of God.*

January 2, 2014 – Vengeance.

I was working on Lesson 22 in A Course In Miracles entitled:
"What I see is a form of vengeance." I found I was blocked on the
notion of vengeance. I did not understand this for I did not feel
vengeful. Intellectually I understood what the lesson was saying
but I could not relate to it experientially. I wanted to understand
the notion of vengeance as it related to me. So I quieted my mind
and I went to my Inner Wisdom and I asked. The following is the
deluge that came forward:

I do not understand the term vengeance as it relates to my
perceptions. I do not feel vengeance most of the time. What I am
in touch with is sadness. Is this a form of vengeance?

*Yes. It is not Love. It is the belief that you have done something
wrong. You believe you separated your awareness from God. So
now you punish yourself. When others remind you of the love that
has been lost you punish them. Is this not vengeance?*

Yes. But I did separate my awareness from God. I am not aware
of his presence in this moment and most moments. My past
experiences of being with God seem to be fading and I cannot
seem to bring the experience back into my awareness.

*Yes this is vengeance. You are punishing yourself and you punish
others when they do not give you the love and understanding you
expect. You know the place where God dwells. You can sense it
now. Your tears tell you of this Truth. It is impossible to believe
this world is real and at the same time accept the experience of
God.*

The veil is thinning for you. Trust in this. Your discontent seems real and you know it is nothing you need to accept as real. It is just a form of vengeance, a form of punishment that you inflict on yourself even when it seems to be directed outwards. Just accept the Truth of God's eternal presence. You know this as Truth and discontent as falsehood. Simply do not accept what is not Truth.

As I did the lesson I felt at peace with the experience and the notion of the impermanence of all things and the vengeance implied in such a world. But as I was moving from object to object I also got a sense of something that is permanent – Love. So after the lesson I tuned inward and continued the dialogue:

I can see the impermanence of everything that surrounds me. But I also sense the Love that emanates from all things.

Yes, this is the call of Love. It is the call to return home where you have never left. It is the promise that you have not forsaken God nor He you. To experience the Love that flows from and between all things is the happy dream. It is still a dream but it brings your awareness closer to the experience of God. This is the thinning of the veil of forgetfulness. In time the veil becomes so thin that the awareness of God can no longer be held back. In this sense you do not take the final step God does.

Thank you as always you bring me peace.

We are one in peace.

January 4, 2014 – Confusion.

I was intrigued by an email from a friend asking why there are so many definitions of terms and opinions' dealing with one's stated relationship to our place in the universe? So I went to my Inner Wisdom and asked. This is the answer that came to me and what I wrote back to my friend:

We are all on a path of self discovery. Who am I and what is my relationship to others? Why am I here? How did I and this world come into being? Is there a God? What do I need to do to be safe and happy? Through time these questions have been asked and answered. But the reality is that the true answer to these questions (Truth) comes to us through experience (revelation) rather then any type of cognitive process. Actually the only thought process that is involved is formulating the question you want answered. Even this does not require words it can be a sense of discontent and a desire to find a better way to live in this world.

The experience of Truth (revelation) often results in the desire to share the experience and the effort is made to translate the experience into a physical form (words, art, dance, music, etc.). We live in a dualistic world and anything that is physical will always have at least two opposing interpretations. Thus as others view the interpretation of the original experience (revelation) there will be misinterpretations. This will be followed by reinterpretations. It is in this way that multiple meanings for the same word, or term, or historical account comes about.

But know that when we view mystical writings or expressions from our ego misinterpretation is assured. When we view from our Heart (we allow the experience of the words to provide the meaning), we can access the Truth that lies within the physical expression (words, art, dance, song). But know this is our Truth by which I mean that Spirit will provide meaning to guide us along our path of self- discovery just as the mystical experience of the original author guided them along their path of self-discovery.

In considering the difference between spirituality and religion, the following is what came through for me: *The focus of spirituality is the self and finding your Truth. Religion tends to be more focused on the community and a doctrine rather than an individual approach to Truth. But know that both can be legitimate paths to Truth or diversions from Truth. What matters is the guide you bring with you - ego centered (our fears) or Heart Centered (Spirit).*

127

As I wrote the above there was one more thing that came to me about the nature of Truth (revelation): Truth is non-dualistic. This is how we know Truth. There is no debate or confusion it is simply known in the moment as Truth. In that moment there simply is no opposite.

Chapter VI
Sacred Words

Within spiritual literature we often see words such as faith, grace, wisdom, love, peace, etc. I call these "Sacred Words" because we tend to use them to describe spiritual experiences. The poems that come through me are liberally sprinkled with these sacred words. A few years back a friend asked me to write about "Hope" and "Grace." This opened up a whole new area of dialogue with that quiet Inner Voice I have come to call Spirit. I began to inquire about the meaning of these sacred words that were so abundant in the poems and wisdom writings that were coming through me. This final chapter contains the poems that came in response to this inquiry.

Hope

Hope is of the Heart.
It springs
from the certainty
of the Love
that surrounds us;
The Oneness
that is at the center
of our Being.

Hope sees the
tragedies of this world,
but knows
there is a stronger force
and a purer vision
that guides us.

Yield to Hope
not despair.

Hope is centered
in your joy
not your pain.

Seek your joy
and there you will find
Hope.

6/29/2009

Grace

*Grace fills you
like the morning sun
on a field of daisies.*

*It has nothing to do with your deeds,
what you think,
or what you strive for.*

*You are a Child of God.
Your perfection remains untainted.*

*What you call grace
emerges into your awareness
when you allow yourself to experience
the Love that surrounds
and fills you.*

*It is Love calling
and reminding you
who you really are.*

*It is a window
into the experience of God
whom you have never
separated from.*

*Grace is the joy in your heart.
It is always there
but is to often hidden
by fear
and the stories you weave
to define and thus limit
who you are.*

On the level of form
Grace is a wonder to behold.
But on the level of Spirit
it is merely
the State of Being.

12/7/2009

Joy

Joy is our purpose
and our guide.

It is not a gift bestowed
upon us
by our deeds or from others.
It is a birthright.

It is an essential quality
of our nature.
For it springs from
the Divine Mother
Whose Love surrounds
and fills us.

Joy is
Love's Companion.

On the level of Spirit
Joy has no opposite.

On the level of the physical
we create barriers to Joy.
It is in this way
we experience discontent.

Discontent is illusion.
Joy is Truth.

Attune yourself to Joy
And it will guide you to itself,
your true self.

12/8/2009

133

Love

Love is
Grace manifested.

Love is to Grace
As warmth is to the sun,
fragrance is to a flower,
and elegance of movement
is to a humming bird.

Like Grace
Love is ever-present
but at times
beyond our awareness.

Every act
at its core is either
the extension of Love
or the call for Love.
There are no exceptions.

On the level of form
Love is often conditional.
This is merely fear
masquerading as Love.
For we have come to believe
that we are not worthy.

But Love is our nature
and its manifestations
surround us.

Open your Heart
to Love's expression
and experience the wonders
that fill your life.

12/14/2009

134

Wonder

Wonder
is the result when we perceive the Divine
reflected in the world around us.

It is the emotion that fills the gap
between our earthly experience and
Spiritual Truth.

It is beyond words or the ability
of our thinking mind to comprehend.

But our Hearts
know Wonder.

Go within to your Magical Child
who will guide you.

Open your Heart.
Release this child.

Let Wonder fill you,
renew you,
guide you.

12/17/2009

Gratitude

Gratitude is
the natural expression of the Heart
when the actions of another or a situation
reminds us who we are:

A Child of God
who is wholly Loved.

We are taught
to believe in limitations.
But deep within us
we know the truth
of our divinity.

Spirit surrounds us
with guides and helpers
to gently lead us back to this truth.

Every moment of every day
is filled with subtle
and sometimes overt
reminders of the Love
that envelops us.

Gratitude opens our awareness
to these signs.

Gratitude is
the extension of Love.
As such
It naturally leads
to Love of self.

136

This is the Path of The Heart.
A path to our True Self.
A path to our
Awakening.

12/18/2009

Wisdom

Like Love
Wisdom is an aspect
of our true nature.

Wisdom is not learned
nor is it gained
through experience
or age.

Learning and experience
only play a role
in helping us remove
the barriers we have constructed
to Wisdom's presence.

As a river wears away stone
to make its path.
Time wears away
our striving for control.

The essential quality
of Wisdom is acceptance.

It is the recognition
that we are guided
by a higher power
that does not exist
outside of our self.

Wisdom flows naturally
when we are attuned
to this inner voice.

It is the voice of
our Higher Self.
Our True Self

It knows our path to
Peace,
Joy,
And Love.

12/20/ 2009

Peace

Peace is
the relinquishment
of our fears.

It is the acceptance
of wisdom
greater than
what can be achieved
through our singular efforts.

It is the precursor
to lasting Joy.

On the level of form
Peace is the space
from which
we come closest
to creating
as God creates.

Often our awareness is such
that Peace seems
beyond our reach.

But know that
Peace is a State of Being.
As such it is ever-present.
Merely turn your thoughts
to this Truth
and allow Peace
to emerge.

12/22/2009

Creation

On the level of form,
creation is the process
of taking an inner state
and expressing it
in a physical form.

On the level of Spirit,
Creation is the
extension of Love.

True Creation
has no limits
and no opposite.

When we
create from the Heart
we come closest to
creating as God Creates.

When we create
from our fears,
our discontent,
what we make
is a false self.

But know that
all efforts at creation,
regardless of the source
represent the process
of self-discovery
and eventually
lead to
Truth.

12/23/2009

Faith

Faith is never lacking.
Every moment of every day
we either put our faith
in the fears that consume us
or the Joy that is ever-present
but often buried
from our awareness.

In this way
faith is merely a decision
to attune our self
to one voice over the other.
The voice of our fears
or the voice of our Joyful Self.
The Voice of Spirit.

Faith in the fearful voice
is always blind
for we choose a veil
that keeps us from seeing
that such faith
is eventually rewarded
with discontent.
There are no exceptions.

Faith in Spirit is at its core
an expression of Love.
Such faith is never blind
for it is always earned.
Peace is the outcome.
There are no exceptions

Many waver
between the two voices.
Thus the cycle
of peace and discontent
is the experience.
There are no exceptions

January 18, 2010

Conclusion

Truth cannot be taught - It can
only be experienced.

We can be taught how to bring
our mind and body into alignment
so that we can differentiate
Truth from falsehood.

Just as the great beauty
perceived through our five senses
is but a pale reflection of the beauty that
resides in each of us, what is taught,
no matter how compelling, is at best only
a shadow of the truth.

By giving any teaching
the status of "truth" we establish a focus
outside of our selves where no truth exists.

Truth which
is synonymous with the Kingdom of Heaven
resides within us.

About the Author

The author and his wife Glenda live in Portland Oregon. They have two grown sons Mathew and Nicholas and two grandsons Felix and Zachary. In 2003 a mystical experience opened him to his spiritual guidance and intuitive abilities. Over the next two years he mentored with a medicine woman in the Lakota Tradition, studied with Sonia Choquette, an internationally renowned psychic and best selling author, and completed advanced certification from the Santa Rosa California School of Alchemical Hypnotherapy. Upon his retirement from social service in November 2004 he started a modest intuitive mentoring practice to help others connect with their inner guidance and intuitive abilities. For more information on the author visit his web site at, http://www.alchemical-transformation-guidance.com/

Made in the USA
San Bernardino, CA
29 October 2014